Contents

KT-226-321

Words written in bold, **like this**, are explained in the Glossary

What are stings and bites?

A sting or a bite is an animal's way of protecting itself. A **hornet**, for example, stings animals that attack it. Sometimes it stings people too.

Other animals use their teeth to bite their enemies. Pets, such as hamsters, are usually happy to be picked up. But they may bite if they are afraid or have babies to protect.

Who gets stings and bites?

Most kinds of **insects** and other animals do not bite or sting. But some insects and other animals bite or sting any person that annoys or alarms them.

You are most likely to be bitten or stung
if you trap or tread on an animal, such as this
scorpion, by mistake. You cannot catch a bite
or sting from another person.

stinging insects

The most common stinging **insects** are wasps and bees. They have a sting at the end of their bodies that they push into your skin.

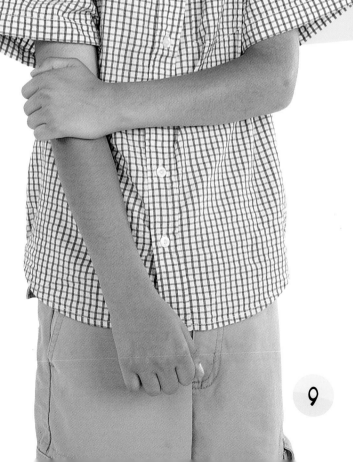

Poison flows down the sting into your flesh. With a bee sting, the sting stays in your flesh and the bee dies soon afterwards.

Jellyfish and sea urchins

Some sea animals use **poison** to defend
themselves or catch **prey**. Jellyfish have stings
on their long **tentacles**. Some jellyfish stings
can harm, or even kill, people.

A **sea urchin** has long, **poisonous** spines to protect itself from being eaten. If you tread on a sea urchin, the spines will stick into your foot.

Mosquitoes

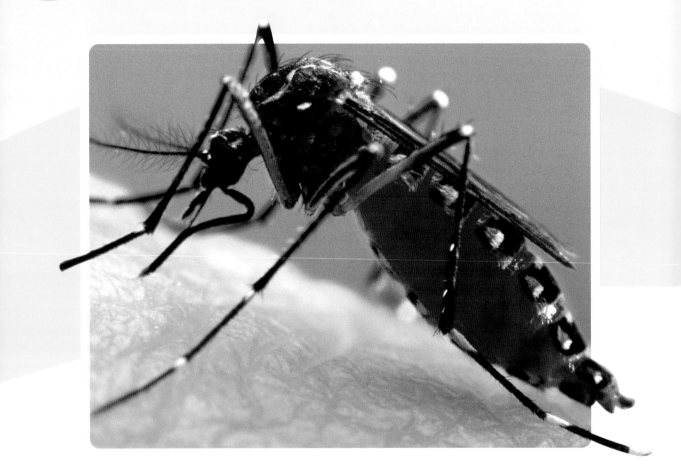

Mosquitoes are one of the most common biting **insects**. Mosquitoes feed on the blood of animals and people. When they bite, they can push **germs** into your body.

In some parts of the world, mosquitoes spread
a dangerous **disease** called **malaria**. A
person catches malaria when they are bitten
by a mosquito that is carrying the disease.

Spiders and snakes

Spiders use their **fangs** to kill their prey.
The bites of a few kinds of spider are so
poisonous they can harm people, or
even kill them.

Some kinds of snake also have a poisonous bite. The snake digs its fangs into its prey. The poison then flows into the victim's blood.

Dogs and other animals

Dogs, cats and other furry animals can bite you if they are alarmed or angry. Pets may bite you by mistake when you are playing with them.

These bites are not **poisonous**, but an animal's teeth are covered in **germs**. If an animal's teeth break your skin, the germs pass through the cut into your blood.

Being stung or bitten

It is easy to tell
when you have
been stung
or bitten by an
insect. Your skin
swells up into a small red lump.
The lump may be itchy or painful.

The swelling is caused by your body's response to the **poison**. A tick is a small animal like a spider. When a tick bites your skin it hangs on. Ask an adult to remove it using tweezers.

Treating minor bites and stings

Most **insect** bites and stings can be treated using a special cream. The cream stops the pain, and the bite or sting heals up after a few days.

If your skin is bleeding, you should tell an adult. Then wash the wound and rub in **antiseptic** cream. If a dog bites you, you may need a **tetanus** injection.

Getting help

Sometimes the **poison** from a serious bite or sting gets into your blood and spreads around your body. If this happens you should phone for medical help.

The poison can affect your **lungs** and make you feel sleepy. It is very important to get help at once if you are bitten by a dog, snake, spider or other dangerous animals.

Antidotes for serious bites and stings

If you have been bitten by a **poisonous** snake or spider, you should see a doctor at once. It will help the doctor if you can describe the snake or spider that bit you.

The doctor or **poison centre** will give you an **antivenom** injection. This is a special medicine that stops the poison from harming you.

Preventing mosquito bites

Mosquitoes come out to hunt when it gets dark. You can spray your skin in the evening with a **chemical** that keeps mosquitoes away.

A special **burner** produces a chemical that drives the mosquitoes out of a closed room. Even better, mosquito nets over the windows or bed stop any mosquitoes from biting you.

Be careful!

You can make sure you are not bitten by some animals by keeping away from them. Do not stroke a strange dog, particularly if it has a bone or puppies.

When you are walking in the countryside, wear strong shoes to protect your feet from being bitten or stung. Look carefully before you pick something up.

Glossary

antiseptic   substance that stops germs growing in number

antivenom   substance that acts against the effect of poison

burner   candle or slow burning coil that makes chemicals that mosquitoes dislike when it is lit

chemical   a powerful substance

disease   illness usually caused by germs

fangs   hollow teeth that are used to inject poison

germs   tiny living things, such as bacteria, that can cause disease if they get inside your body

hornet   type of wasp

infected   diseased area caused by germs getting in

insect   small animal with six legs and three parts to its body

lungs   parts of the body that air goes into when you breathe in

malaria   disease spread by mosquitoes in
   some countries

mosquito   type of insect that feeds on the
   blood of animals and humans

poison   substance that is harmful to the body

poison centre   place where information about
   poisons is given

poisonous   carrying poison

prey   animal that is eaten by another animal

sea urchin   animal that lives in the sea and has
   poisonous spines

tentacles   long feelers

tetanus   infectious disease that affects
   the muscles

More books to read

Really Wild: Snakes, Claire Robinson,
   (Heinemann Library, 1999)
Safe and Sound: Safety First, Angela Royston,
   (Heinemann Library, 2000)

Index